COUNTRY · EXPLORERS

A Visit to

GERMANY

By Rebecca Phillips-Bartlett

BEARPORT
PUBLISHING

Minneapolis, Minnesota

Credits

All images are courtesy of Shutterstock.com, unless otherwise specified. With thanks to Getty Images, Thinkstock Photo, and iStockphoto.

Cover – Oksana Trautwein, canadastock. 2–3 – canadastock. 4–5 – geogif, ixpert. 6–7 – QQ7, canadastock. 8–9 – LALS STOCK, canadastock, pio3. 10–11 – canadastock, Sina Ettmer Photography. 12–13 – HappyRichStudio, Harald Schmidt. 14–15 – trabantos, P Gregory. 16–17 – Vasilika, aldorado. 18–19 – Feel good studio, Free_styler. 20–21 – Rick Kessinger, Dmitry SKilkov. 22–23 – Juergen Wackenhut, mary416.

Library of Congress Cataloging-in-Publication Data is available at www.loc.gov or upon request from the publisher.

ISBN: 979-8-88509-971-4 (hardcover)
ISBN: 979-8-88822-150-1 (paperback)
ISBN: 979-8-88822-291-1 (ebook)

© 2024 BookLife Publishing
This edition is published by arrangement with BookLife Publishing.

For more information, write to Bearport Publishing, 5357 Penn Avenue South, Minneapolis, MN 55419.

CONTENTS

COUNTRY TO COUNTRY

A country is an area of land marked by **borders**. The people in each country have their own rules and ways of living. They may speak different languages.

Which country do you live in?

Each country around the world has its own interesting things to see and do. Let's take a trip to visit a country and learn more!

Have you ever visited another country?

TODAY'S TRIP IS TO GERMANY!

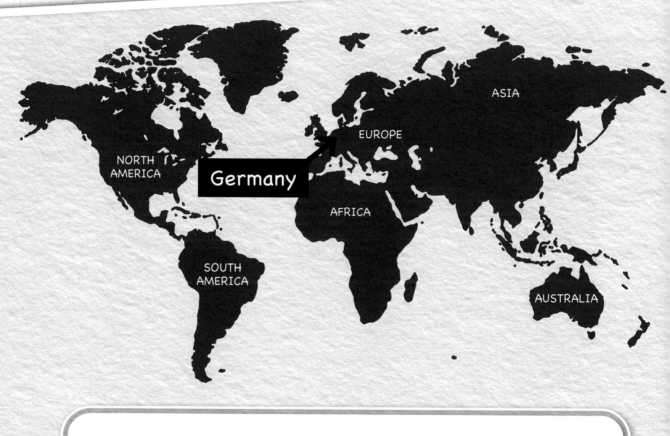

ASIA

EUROPE

NORTH AMERICA

Germany

AFRICA

SOUTH AMERICA

AUSTRALIA

Germany is a country in the **continent** of Europe.

FACT FILE

Capital city: Berlin
Main language: German
Currency: Euro
Flag:

Currency is the type of money that is used in a country.

BERLIN

We'll start our trip in Berlin. It is the country's capital and biggest city. Berlin has a lot of history. It is home to Museum Island.

Museum Island has five museums.

The Berlin Wall

Starting in 1949, Germany was divided into two countries. The Berlin Wall was built to stop people moving between the two. In 1991, the wall was torn down. The country came back together.

CASTLES

Germany
has more
castles than
any other
country in
the world.

Germany has more than 25,000 castles. We might recognize some of them. The Neuschwanstein castle **inspired** many famous fairy tales!

The Landgrafenschloss castle in the city of Marburg also inspired stories. The Brothers Grimm went to school in Marburg. Later, they wrote "Cinderella," "Rapunzel," and many more fairy tales.

MUSIC

Berlin Concert Hall

Next, let's listen to some **classical** music. Beethoven, Bach, and Brahms are some of the most famous German musicians who made this style of music.

An oompah band

Many people in Germany like **folk** music, too. Some of the most popular kinds are oompah, yodeling, and schlager.

COLOGNE CATHEDRAL

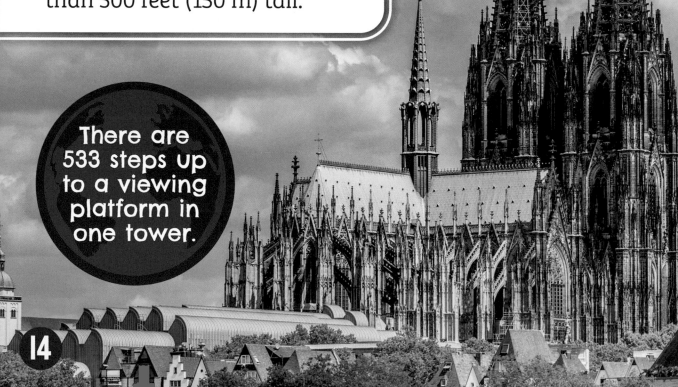

Cologne **Cathedral** took more than 600 years to build. It has two towers that are each more than 500 feet (150 m) tall.

There are 533 steps up to a viewing platform in one tower.

Cologne Cathedral is one of the most visited places in Germany. It is home to the Shrine of the Three Wise Men. Many people visit it on a **pilgrimage**.

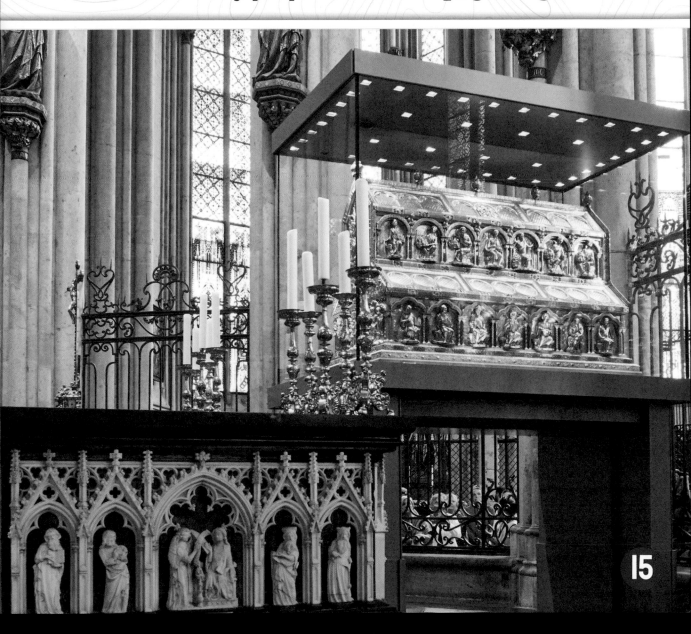

RACING

Motorsports are popular in Germany. The country has a long history of making cars. There are many museums about cars.

Western Germany has a famous racetrack called the Nürburgring. Before it was built, all car races took place on public roads. The Nürburgring made racing much safer.

CHRISTMAS IN GERMANY

Striezelmarkt has been around for nearly 600 years. It is Germany's oldest Christmas market.

Ready for some shopping? Many cities in Germany have special markets around Christmas. There are lots of things to buy and eat. One of the most famous Christmas markets is Dresden's Striezelmarkt.

The town of Rothenburg ob der Tauber is full of Christmas all year. It is home to a Christmas village and a Christmas museum.

FOOD

Feeling hungry? Let's grab some food. First, we'll try some of Germany's famous sausages. The country has more than 1,200 different types. The most popular are bratwurst sausages.

Bratwurst sausages

Pretzels are another popular German food. They are usually twisted and shaped into knots.

Pretzels are often sold as street food.

BEFORE YOU GO

We can't forget to visit the Black Forest! This place has beautiful trees and mountains. There is an open-air museum here.

We could also drive along the Fairy Tale Route. It is about 370 miles (600 km) long. We might see places that inspired Rapunzel's tower, Little Red Riding Hood's house, or even Snow White's castle.

What have you learned about Germany on this trip?

GLOSSARY

borders lines that show where one place ends and another begins

cathedral a very large church

classical a traditional type of music often played by a large orchestra

continent one of the world's seven large land masses

folk music traditional music of the people in a country

inspired gave ideas about something

motorsports sports that involve racing or driving cars

pilgrimage a religious journey

INDEX